Robert
Burns Night

A freestyle guide

Boyd Baines

Saraband

CONTENTS

'A Scottish Bard, Proud of the Name'
INTRODUCTION

If an evening of ceilidh-dancing, whisky-drinking and kilt-flashing sounds like your kind of party – and, let's face it, why wouldn't it be? – then you've come to the right book. Burns Night is one of the great celebrations of the year. That's because Robert Burns (1759–96) – in his personality, his poems and song and his 'Immortal Memory' – stands for so much of what makes life worthwhile... and for what makes it fun.

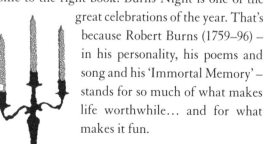

EXTRAORDINARILY ORDINARY

Why commemorate a poet, however great? That is, if we're not ourselves generally literary in our interests or activities? We don't have Gerard Manley Hopkins Hoedowns, Shakespeare celebrations or Shelley suppers. Not too many of us mark Milton's birthday, or commemorate Keats in any way at all.

But Burns was no ordinary poet. Or rather, he *was* an ordinary poet – you could hardly have found anyone more ordinary than this Ayrshire farmworker who nevertheless went on to attain the heights of beauty and sophistication in his poems. He even managed to achieve this without losing touch with the world around him – that was the other extraordinary thing about him; the way he kept faith with the simpler things in life even as he wrestled with the big intellectual, political and poetic issues.

A rose and a revolution; Scotland's destiny and that of a wounded hare; tyranny and toothache: Burns was equally at ease addressing all these things. A mouse; a louse; a young man's swearing; a ploughman's toil; a witches' sabbath: Burns could find the poetry – and the wit – in everything. The delights of love; the wrench of separation; the absurdities of snobbery; the outrage of injustice… It's hard to think of an aspect of experience he didn't get to grips with in his poems.

THE PEOPLE'S PARTY

It's more than this, though. 'Rabbie' Burns isn't remembered now just for some of Scottish (and world) literature's most unforgettable works. The self-styled 'Scottish Bard' has endured as a man – almost as a friend. Even in death, he's so much larger than life, famous as a lover, a fighter, a patriot and a radical, an impulsive champion of the poor and the oppressed.

But Burns' sense of social solidarity didn't stop at high-minded discussion. Unlike so many other radicals, whose humanitarianism can seem abstract and theoretical, Burns felt a strong and spirited bond with his fellow man. (And, of course, with womankind – to a controversial extent sometimes, though over time his romantic shenanigans have simply added to the myth.)

Naebody ever ca'd me Rabbie

Though never really party-political, the poet was very definitely a party animal – with what he himself described as 'a strong appetite for sociability'. He loved to laugh and joke; to tease and flirt; to sing, swap gossip, eat, drink and dance.

A SCOTTISH CELEBRATION

In short, a bit of bashfulness aside (given the glowing tributes to his poetic greatness and personal charm), he'd have liked nothing better than the Burns Supper of today. That's just about as ringing an endorsement as the institution could receive.

Burns Night isn't all about Rabbie, though. Done properly, it's a spirited celebration of Scottish culture as a whole: all sorts of colourful traditions get an outing over the evening. It's not just the Scottish food and drink – there's the kilt and there's the ceilidh (pronounced 'kay-lee'), where the guests are able to dance off all the haggis, neeps and tatties at the end of the night. There can be innumerable other enjoyable Caledonian touches, too.

5

Along with the Burns Night smartphone app, this book is your one-stop shop for all things Burns Night – everything is here, from the poems to the place settings, from the biographical background to the toasts. Whether you're a winsome wee novice looking for the basic running order or a grizzled auld veteran after interesting changes and tweaks, you'll find information and enlightenment – and, we hope, a bit of fun. Read right through or just dip and browse as you want: you'll find everything clearly and simply set out, with an emphasis on what is practical and on what works. In no time at all, you'll be raring to go, ready to raise your glass tae Rabbie Burns – the Scottish Bard, and an inspiration to the world.

Weel spotted – this isnae me, but folk expect Hielan' tartan in a Scottish book

'The Best-laid Schemes o' Mice and Men'
HISTORY OF ROBERT BURNS

Robert Burns was born on 25th January, 1759, on a small farm just outside Alloway, in southern Ayrshire. His parents, William Burnes and Agnes Broun (or Brown), were poor: William was a tenant, and didn't own 'his' land. They did what they could for their son. His father gave him some sort of basic schooling (he'd supplement that later, intermittently, at a local village school), but his formal education was patchy, to say the least.

Agnes, it's said, loved to sing and tell stories and encouraged the same love in young Rabbie. He was by no means without intellectual or imaginative stimulation in his early years, then. But, as a farmer's son, all he could realistically look forward to was a life sentence of hard labour. The burden he had to carry for the sake of his family was almost literally crippling – even in early boyhood, there were signs that his health was suffering. By fifteen, he was the principal labourer on his parents' farm.

'GIE ME AE SPARK O' NATURE'S FIRE'

A young man in his position had little alternative but to accept his lot – but Burns was rebelling inwardly, that much is clear. Everything we know of him at this time suggests that he had resolved that somehow he would live, even if it killed him.

Though all but crushed by the rigours of his working day, he found the energy from somewhere to walk out around Alloway and steep himself in the knowledge of his native countryside. He got to know its people too, laughing and drinking with its young men and romancing its girls. While he was to win his fame primarily as a poet – and he was a writer of immense intellectual sophistication and technical skill – his works would have been nothing without his love of nature and his instinctive understanding of human life.

Despite his comparative lack of learning, and the disdain he expressed for the sort of scholarship that came out of books and leisured privilege, he did his best to make up his deficit, and was a tireless reader. Along, of course, with the Bible, he's known to have read verse and prose in Latin and in French – and English poetry: works by Shakespeare, Dryden, Milton and many more.

OUT OF AYRSHIRE

Quite when he started writing isn't clear, but in 1786, when he was twenty-seven, his first book was published, by John Wilson, who had a printing firm in Kilmarnock. Burns had been on the point of emigrating, his passage booked to Jamaica, when this publication convinced him he might still have a future in Scotland.

Comprised of beautiful love lyrics, good-humoured satires and thoughtful philosophical reflections, what's now known as the Kilmarnock Edition was actually entitled *Poems Chiefly in the Scottish Dialect*. There's no doubt that – as this title suggests – Burns' poems piqued curiosity in part because they were written in Scots, a language till then widely disdained as 'low' and intrinsically un-literary. Nor is there any doubt that Burns himself was patronised as a 'Ploughman Poet'.

But then, Burns was happy to play up to that image himself. 'The Poetic Genius of my country found me… at the plough', he said in the Preface to his Kilmarnock collection: 'She bade me sing the loves, the joys, the rural scenes and rural pleasures of my native soil, in my native tongue.' Patronising it may have been, then, but Rabbie Burns was not complaining. It beat backbreaking work in the fields, that's for sure. The Kilmarnock Edition was successful and proved to be his ticket out of Ayrshire. Within a year, he had moved to Edinburgh and published his second book of poems, whilst dabbling in various romances along the way.

BURNING LOVE

'Burnsmania' certainly did not do anything to diminish the poet's attraction to women, but his pre-dilection for the fairer sex had been well established in his native Ayrshire long before his fame. He and

Jean Armour – the nearest thing he had to a long-term girlfriend – had even been hauled up before Alloway's Kirk Elders and ordered to make a public apology after she fell pregnant.

All told, Burns was to father thirteen children by five different women. His philandering reputation was to become essential to his mythic charisma. But it was every bit as essential to his work. His poems pleaded, cajoled and, if all went well, finally seduced the women to whom they were addressed. His conquests in their turn inspired his writing.

It was a married woman, who signed her love letters to Burns with the name 'Clarinda', that inspired the splendid verses of 'Ae Fond Kiss'. Ae fond kiss may well have been all he got from 'Clarinda'. She was in fact Mrs Agnes Maclehose, a beautiful young Edinburgh woman, who was separated from her husband, and seems to have loved the young poet – but, unfortunately for him, it appears she loved her social status and reputation that bit more.

Generally, the evidence suggests that Burns' romantic record was as long as your arm, but there's no evidence that he was a cold or calculating user.

His ardour may have been fleeting but – while it lasted – it was blazingly sincere.

DAZZLING SKILL, DECLINING HEALTH

The more you read Burns' poetry, though, the clearer it becomes that – whatever he felt for the women in his life – his first love was his language. His simplest, most naïve-seeming lyrics are minor miracles of balance and weight; longer poems like 'Tam o' Shanter' take the breath away with their exuberant inventiveness and dazzling skill. They're great literature – as well as being hugely entertaining.

Sadly, Burns was destined to burn out with tragic speed despite the fact that he appeared to have settled down. By 1789, he'd moved to Dumfries and resumed his on-going relationship with the long-suffering Jean Armour, whom he'd married formally the year before. Thanks to a powerful patron, he had a new and less physically punishing job as an excise officer. But the damage had been done already, and his health declined with alarming speed. On 21st July, 1796, he died, aged just thirty-seven.

'A RIGHT GUID WILLIE-WAUGHT'

On 25th January, 1801, on what would have been Burns' birthday, a dinner was held in his honour by nine of his friends at Burns Cottage. It was to be the first of a long succession of celebration suppers, the key elements of which really haven't changed much in 200-odd years. There remains the best of Scottish food and drink; the toast to the Immortal Memory; the recitations of Burns' work – and an energetic ceilidh to conclude.

Remembrance is at the heart of a tradition that was conceived to commemorate an absent but still-beloved friend. Since that friend, with songs like *Auld Lang Syne*, had made himself pretty much a laureate of nostalgia, Burns Night became an ideal opportunity for whisky-assisted retrospection on an enjoyably sentimentalised, red, red rose-tinted past. And given Burns' status as 'Scottish Bard', with his stirring songs of patriotism and his more tender poems of exile, it was understandable that emigrants around the world (and their descendants) should have come to see the Burns Supper as an important celebration of who they were.

Whoever, wherever you are, though, this festival of friendship, conviviality, wit and raucous fun, can be among the most joyous nights of the year. The little effort it takes to make it a success is worth it, every time...

'The Mirth and Fun Grew Fast and Furious'
BURNS NIGHT RUNNING ORDER

Poetry, food, drink, dance, dressing up, witty speeches, music, toasts to friends: Burns Night is about all these things and more. Exactly where each element comes in the scale of importance will of course depend on you, where your interests and priorities lie, and what you're hoping to get out of your celebration.

If you and your friends are musicians, you might rustle up a fairly serious ceilidh band; you could also hook up your phone to speakers and play music from the Burns Night app. A university literature department's Burns bash might be a bit more ambitious in its choice of recitations, more erudite in its speeches maybe. If you're fans of fashion or students of textile design, this is your chance to go to town on tartan and black velvet; if you love cooking, the meal may be the most important thing for you.

It really doesn't matter: Burns Night can accommodate all these different emphases. It can be customised to just about any format you want, in fact. As long as the key components are there, Burns Night can be endlessly adapted – the traditional running order doesn't have to be slavishly adhered to. Make your Burns Supper as unique and personal as you wish, omitting or adding elements to the evening. Using veggie haggis, banning booze, forgetting the ceilidh, introducing games to the proceedings – anything goes!

The full, traditional running order of the Burns Supper is shown overleaf.

The Selkirk Grace
Serve the starter
Pipe the haggis in
Address to a Haggis
Serve the haggis
Serve the main course
Serve the dessert
Serve cheese and biscuits
Have coffee and a wee dram
Thanks and special speeches
The Immortal Memory
Tam o' Shanter
Toast to the Lassies
Reply from the Lassies
Burns songs
Pipe medley
Ceilidh
Auld Lang Syne

Which of these items you choose to highlight and which to play down (or even drop completely) is entirely up to you. After all, Burns Night is your night, too. *Ah'm the star, mind*

'Drouthy Neebors, Neebors Meet'
SETTING THE MOOD

Wherever your supper is held, presentation – the way you set out the table and the room – is absolutely crucial in creating the right kind of mood. The trick is to combine formality and fun: the former because there has to be the feeling that this is an occasion for which it's worth making a bit of an effort, sartorially and socially; the latter because – well, having a great time is what Burns Night is ultimately about.

TARTAN TRAPPINGS

Ideally, dress code and decoration should complement each other. Burns Night is about community and conviviality, so it shouldn't be a fashion arms race: look good, by all means, but there should be the sense of a common goal. Realistically, this means a traditionally Scottish look, and that in turn probably means tartan – though that's not necessarily anything like as restrictive as it may sound. Tartan comes in numerous designs and colours, and these days it's not just limited to those of the different clans. How much you use in your Burns Night decor depends on your personal taste.

Tartan is almost as divisive, aesthetically, as bagpipe music: for some people a little goes a long, long way, while for others there can be no such thing as 'too much'. Rejecting tartan altogether does seem self-defeating, though. Like it or not, nothing says 'Scotland' so instantly or unmistakeably; and, with so many different patterns and colours on offer, you should be able to find at least one tartan that you like.

Tartan table runners, tablecloths, and napkins are widely available in shops, although there may be more variety and choice online. If you are particularly determined to keep everything strictly Burns, you could find an alternative to tartan (see pages 22–23 for more on the tartan). Thistles, to coin a phrase, 'll do.

'AND A' THAT...'

There's no doubt that most people will feel that, when the hall's decked with too much tartan, the effect can become monotonous – if not actually over-whelming. It's always worth ringing the changes a bit. Centrepieces based on saltires or lions rampant, displays of heather or thistles (or other distinctively Scottish plants) will provide a splash of lively colour to the table and keep the flavour good and Scottish.

Try hanging some flags around the room: don't just focus on the Saint Andrew's Cross; an array of other nations' flags will emphasise the inclusivity of Burns Night. (Burns may have been a patriot, but he was also an internationalist, and his celebration is certainly not just for Scots.) Details such as these can be used to break up a predominantly tartan decora-tive scheme.

Place cards done in the style of Burns' signature may add a literary note to proceedings, especially if you inscribe a line of verse on each one. If you're having a particularly grand supper, naming the different tables after some of Rabbie's best known poems might be an nice touch.

For an authentic feel, a crackling fire gives a cosy glow to the room: Burns would have written his poems by this sort of warm and flickering light. If your venue doesn't have a fireplace, candles offer a nice atmospheric alternative. Be sure not to start a fire, though, once the whisky starts flowing!

These are just suggestions, of course – you can organise these things the way you want them, set the mood according to your own tastes. That's the best way to summon up that special Burns Night ambience.

'Her Cutty-sark, o' Paisley Harn'
WHAT TO WEAR

Key elements of the contemporary Burns Supper are – quite unashamedly – 'invented tradition'. Yet, they were adopted so long ago now that they're effectively 'true' traditions, too. The (male) dress code is the most controversial. Strictly 'Highland' in style, it consists of the kilt, of course; the sporran; the short 'Bonnie Prince Charlie' jacket; the woollen socks with garter-flashes; and, for the really serious, the *sgian dubh*: the Highland dirk or dagger, thrust down into the sock.

FORBIDDEN FABRIC

As 'Burns Supper specialist' Clark McGinn has pointed out, however, Burns himself, an Ayrshire Lowlander of the eighteenth century, would never have dreamed of wearing these items. Even if he had ever wanted to, moreover, he would have been strictly forbidden from doing so by law. The Dress Act, passed after Bonnie Prince Charlie's Jacobite Rebellion of 1745 – one of a series of measures introduced in an effort to suppress the old clan culture of the Highlands – explicitly banned the wearing of such gear. It was repealed in 1782, by which time the threat from the Stuart claimants to Britain's throne was seen to have subsided.

Meanwhile, Sir Walter Scott's best-selling novels and poems had popularised a new, non-threatening form of 'Scottishness', which brought together Highland and Lowland motifs indiscriminately – everything from sporrans to shortbread. Knock it if you like (and Scottish intellectuals routinely do) but Scott's sentimental Caledonian cocktail still helps form the basis of the country's contemporary identity, providing Scotland with a strong sense of its own cultural individuality (and attracting a never-ending stream of foreign tourists).

The establishment of this identity, however dubious, led to the 'tradition' of there being a uniform tartan for every clan – and, ultimately, for a great many other groups as well. Burns' admirers are no exception. After all, if the Detroit Police Department can have its own tartan, why shouldn't Scotland's Bard?

Surprisingly, perhaps, it was not until 2009 that the Robert Burns Legacy tartan came into being, brought in to mark the 250th anniversary of the Bard's birth. Even by the standards of the tartan pretend-tradition, then, the Robert Burns Legacy is a 'parvenu-plaid' – very much a newcomer on the scene. It's still well worth supporting, though. In the first place because it looks good, and in the second place because a contribution goes to the Robert Burns Birthplace Museum with every item sold. It's also true to the Burns Night spirit in fusing the past with the present, the authentic with the ersatz, the bringing together of high-minded literariness with good, clean fun. *This book's dress'd in Legacy colours tae —*

FOR HONEST MEN...

Your Burns Night, your rules: there's certainly no law that says men should have to show up in Prince Charlie jackets, kilts and cross-laced brogues and all the other doings. There can be quite a bit of expense and trouble if they do.

Before you dispense with a traditional dress code, though, think how much you might stand to lose in atmosphere and the sense of occasion. Remember, too, that men who in anticipation feel nothing but dread and embarrassment at the thought of going out in what amounts to a skirt, often find when the time comes that they're really glad they made the effort, their kilt concerns quickly banished by the Burns Night spirit.

When you've made that commitment to the event, it's somehow so much easier to get into the Burns Night mood, and so much more enjoyable when you do. That's before we even get to the fact that, if everyone else has come kilted, you might easily end up feeling conspicuous if you don't.

... AND BONNIE LASSES

There's no comparable code of dress for women and girls. They have the freedom to decide for themselves what they will wear. And, of course, the hassle and the headache that go with that. Basically, it makes sense to make an effort – whatever that means to you – and then add whatever Scottish touches you may choose (a sprig of heather, some appropriate jewellery). Don't forget too, that you want something you can feel comfortable dancing in.

MAKE IT CLEAR

To conclude with a caution: up to now we've been banging on about the importance of an easy-going approach to Burns Night, urging you to customise your supper as you see fit. But given the potential for misunderstanding – and consequent embarrassment – it *is* up to you as host or hostess to be explicit in issuing some sort of dress code with your invitation, so your guests have a good idea what you expect. It's not just the success of your evening that depends on it, but also the ability of your guests to relax and enjoy it. The guy who's frightened of feeling conspicuous in a kilt might all too easily find himself looking like a proper numpty in a classic black-tie dinner suit; or else strolling up in a hoodie, T-shirt and jeans.

'Food fills the wame, an' keeps us livin'
FOOD AND DRINK

The Burns Supper classically centres on the main event: the presentation of the haggis. Yet there are many other dishes you can include on the menu if

25

you like. Even the haggis is up for reinvention: it's possible nowadays to find vegetarian versions of what was always very much a meat-based treat.

SUPERLATIVE SOUPS

Soup is the best way to start the evening, literally warming up your guest after their journey to your home through all the rigours of the January chill (at least, in the Northern Hemisphere). Scotch broth is the obvious candidate, with its long patriotic pedigree – and a barley content that's popularly believed to help soak up the booze.

But then Cock-a-leekie (or 'Cockyleekie') soup is just as Caledonian: as its name suggests, it's made from chicken and leeks and it's both hearty and nutritious. Originally, a few prunes were included as well: cut some into strips and add to each dish before serving and you have a traditional touch that even seems a bit exotic nowadays. For a fishy alternative, there's Cullen Skink, a delicious and surprisingly subtle concoction of smoked haddock, potatoes and onions. It's just the thing to get your guests into the festive spirit.

KNOW YOUR NEEPS

Then it's time for the ceremonial serving of the haggis. Whether the traditional or vegetarian version, the haggis should come with the customary 'bashit neeps' and 'chappit tatties'. 'Neep', as you might well have guessed, is a contraction of the word 'turnip' – but beware: the Scots turnip is what the English call a 'swede'.

One root crop, you might think, is much like another, but the neep or swede is not only a great deal bigger, typically, than the turnip: there's also a surprising amount of difference in taste and texture. Most people find the firmer, orangey-yellow flesh of the swede a lot nicer to eat than that of the classic English turnip, which is white and (some say) slimy, and doesn't really taste of very much. Certainly the swede seems to complement the haggis and tatties superbly.

The neeps are traditionally 'bashit' – mashed up with butter; as, for that matter, are the 'Chappit tatties', to all intents and purposes what the English would call 'mashed potato' or 'mash'.

WHISKY OR WINE? *Or Buckie, beer, or 'Bru?*

Usually, too, it's appropriate to pour guests a wee dram of single malt whisky to toast the haggis with at the conclusion of the 'Address to a Haggis', which is always read out loud (or, ideally, recited) at this point. Malt may seem extortionately expensive by comparison with the more readily available blended brands. And it is – but with very good reason, you'll find. Regular whisky may be fine of an evening with a splash of soda or ginger ale, but it's not fit company for a noble haggis. A fine, mature malt slips down smoothly, while its complex taste brings out the full richness of the Burns Night meal.

Whisky – however upmarket – isn't everybody's favourite cup of alcohol. It's been suggested that a French claret goes better with this course – and might even be more authentic, historically, if that matters. Ultimately, it's up to you: Burns Night is often a family affair and you might well have views on how much or how little alcohol you might wish to see served – especially in the lead-up to the speeches!

MAIN COURSE MATTERS

When it comes to haggis, you could make the whole thing yourself from scratch – but it's a serious foodie who wants to spend several hours up to his or her elbows in all that offal, oatmeal and suet. By all means do that if you enjoy the challenge, but there's really no shame in taking the easy way out and buying a pre-packaged haggis, especially as it's possible to buy some very high quality products these days. Many shops can supply both the traditional haggis and a vegetarian option, so there's something for everyone (source online if you're not in Scotland).

If you don't like the idea of haggis, in either its meat or vegetarian form, then there are plenty of other options available. Obviously, it makes things feel more authentic when your main course is based on something recognisably Scottish: salmon or Aberdeen Angus beef – or even, if you're feeling flush and want to push the boat out, venison or grouse. All these dishes can be served with plenty of tatties on the side. For added decadence you can serve up your main course (and this goes for haggis also) with a creamy whisky sauce.

JUST DESSERTS

If your guests aren't full by this time, you can guarantee they will be by the time they've managed to get through a serving of Cranachan – perhaps the richest pudding known to man. Anyone who thinks the Scots are 'dour' or joyless has never sampled this dessert of whisky-soaked oatmeal, raspberries and heather honey, dished up (generally in a glass – prawn cocktail-style) with whisky and whipped cream. Calvinism and calorie-consciousness alike go out of the window when the Cranachan is brought in: this dish is pretty much the definition of excess. Tipsy Laird (or 'trifle', as the English would call it, Scotsed up with a dash of Drambuie, instead of sherry) looks positively austere by comparison.

For those indefatigable diners who still have room, you can bring in a selection of Scottish cheeses – served up, it goes without saying, with oatcakes. Scotland produces some of the finest cheeses in the world, including some splendid cheddars, such as the sharp-edged whites from the Isle of Mull. Caboc, a subtle-tasting cream cheese, comes coated in oatmeal, for maximum Scottishness, but there are other fabulous cream cheeses, like Crowdie and Howgate Highland. For an uncompromising blue cheese, try Lanark Blue or Dunsyre – the first made with ewe's milk; the second with cow's. Or there's Brodick Blue from the Isle of Arran – again, there's a cow's milk equivalent, simply called Brodick. Really, though, the list is endless: shop around and see what you can find, as new artisan cheeses are becoming available (and old ones rediscovered) all the time.

You can, if you really want to, get seriously serious about your oatcakes, too. Oatcake enthusiasts give real ale buffs a run for their money. Briefly, the 'rougher', the more coarsely-ground the meal, the more high-end the product. In many of the most popular brands, the oatmeal is mixed with wheat flour – to the outrage of the true aficionado. Such mongrel products can't be genuinely 'authentic', so the argument goes (even if they have been happily scoffed by the Scots themselves for generations).

After the cheese and oatcakes, it's time to sit back and enjoy some coffee (or possibly wine or whisky!) in preparation for the speeches.

Ye can finish wi' a snowball or tablet

There are countless other recipes that can chime with the main traditions of Burns Suppers. To get your culinary imagination and appetite going, look up recipes on the food and drink pages of VisitScotland's website, or try specialist haggis sites such as Macsween's or Grant's Haggis.

'Be thankit'
THE SELKIRK GRACE

Scandalous in his conduct and sceptical in his thinking, Burns couldn't have been said to be on the most cordial of terms with the Scottish Kirk. He was free and outspoken in his satirising of what he saw as religious hypocrisy and cant. Yet he was a firm believer in the brotherhood of humankind. When he was called upon to say grace at a dinner given by the Earl of Selkirk in 1793, he offered this prayer:

Some hae meat and canna eat,
And some wad eat that want it;
But we hae meat, and we can eat,
And sae let the Lord be thankit.

It's often assumed that the Selkirk Grace was Burns' own composition, improvised on the spot; but it is in fact a familiar prayer of the time. It's easy enough to see why it would have appealed to this most secular of spirits, though, and why it should have become an indispensable prelude to the traditional Burns Night meal.

'The Piper Loud and Louder Blew'
BAGPIPES

There's nothing like the sound of the bagpipe… and God be thankit for small mercies, some will say. It's not universally beloved, that's for sure. According to Shylock in *The Merchant of Venice*, there are some people who 'when the bagpipe sings i' the nose, cannot contain their urine'. But then what did Shakespeare know? However fainthearted the Bard of Avon may have been, the Scottish Bard would have expected his enthusiasts to be made of sterner stuff. And so, you'll inevitably find, they are. Not only will your guests succeed in maintaining bladder control, most will find the pipes enjoyable – exhilarating, even. At traditional Burns Suppers, the guests are always welcomed with the sound of bagpipes, as is the evening's guest of honour, the haggis.

THE SOUND OF SCOTLAND

Bagpipes are seen as quintessentially Scottish, emblematic of the nation, but their first appearance appears to have been in the Middle East. Archaeological researchers have found 3,000-year-old evidence that the pipes were first played not by Highlanders but by Hittites, in the mountains of Turkey. Regional variations from subsequent centuries appear here and there across western Asia and North Africa, as well as on the continent of Europe.

The bagpipes (in Gaelic *a' phìob mhòr*) certainly have been played for many centuries in Scotland, but their adoption as a patriotic symbol is more recent.

They gained this status, ironically, with the expansion of the British Empire. Scottish soldiers played a key role in the empire-building effort from the eighteenth century onwards: if the great Highland regiments were Britain's shock troops, the bagpipes were their secret weapon. The sheer volume of the skirling pipes; the nerve-shredding edge of the high notes; the relentless drone: all these intimidated enemies, whilst simultaneously stirring morale on the British side.

MIXOLYDIAN MUSIC

A contemporary set of pipes contains a blowpipe and a bag (for containing and controlling the air flow). A chanter plays the melodic line, while there are two tenor drones and a bass drone. A vibrating reed in each of these produces the sound. The chanter is tuned to the Mixolydian mode, whose flattened 7th, or leading note, lends an eerie distinctiveness to the typical bagpipe tune. Bagpipe music, its melody heard above the hum of the accompanying drones, is especially evocative out in the open, where the vibrating tones will resonate most strongly.

If you don't play the pipes personally, or are unable to source a bagpiper for the job, you can download the Burns Night app. This features a professionally recorded bagpipe tune – perfect for piping in the guests and the haggis. Alternatively, there are countless CDs you can pick up that are also a decent alternative to the real thing. The sound of the bagpipes revving up to play creates the buzz every successful Burns Night needs, and puts everybody in the mood to party.

'Great Chieftain o' the Puddin-race!'
THE HAGGIS

'Wha's like us?' the Scots ask, rhetorically. In one respect, at least, it's a real question: what other nation gives a boiled grain and offal pudding pride of place at its greatest feast? What the turkey is to the USA's Thanksgiving or the lamb to the Jewish Passover, the haggis is to the traditional Burns Supper. It seems perverse – or would do, at any rate, if you'd never come in from the cold and damp of a dreich January evening to tuck into haggis with tatties and neeps, with a nip of whisky. Once you have, you'll appreciate just how inspired a tradition it really is. What better way to keep the winter chill at bay? And what a noble texture and what a regal taste this unpromising mess of lowly ingredients turns out to have: 'great chieftain o' the puddin-race' indeed.

But what *is* the haggis?

FIRST, CATCH YOUR HAGGIS

Scottish butchers like to joke about 'freshly caught' or 'free range' haggis, as though these were little animals grazing hillside fields or roaming wild. They make a show of secrecy around their recipes when, in fact, there is little mystery about it – even if considerable skill is involved in making it really well. Briefly, haggis consists of sheep's 'pluck' (offal), which is mixed with stock, spices, onion, oatmeal and suet. Traditionally simmered for three hours in the lining of the sheep's stomach, it is today more often sold in artificial casing or sausage casing.

For those put off by such ingredients, vegetarian options are widely available – and frequently work well. *Hagese*, to give it its Gaelic name, is not even necessarily entirely Scottish in its origins. The earliest recipe we have comes from the 1430 Lancashire cookbook, *Liber Cure Cocorom*.

THE MOMENT OF TRUTH

There's no disputing, though, that the Scots have made the dish their own, the traditional centrepiece of any Burns Supper. It is given a reception fit for a chieftain, borne in on a large platter and preceded by a bagpiper. A speaker now starts declaiming Burns' magnificently stirring 'Address to a Haggis', all the while cleaning and sharpening his or her knife in readiness to carve. Raising it up in readiness at the line *'His knife see rustic Labour dight'*, he or she then holds the knife histrionically poised, waiting for the line 'An' cut ye up wi' ready slight' before plunging it into the haggis, opening it up to an awestruck company. A truly impressive spectacle to behold.

ADDRESS TO A HAGGIS

One of Burns' most famous poems, the 'Address to a Haggis' is also one of his most skilfully contrived, at once a witty sally and a patriotic boast. It's also paradoxically dramatic – given its humble subject – encapsulating the sense of occasion, the mounting anticipation and the climactic theatricality of the knife plunging in to pierce the haggis' encasing skin in a veritable eruption of 'reekin' steam:

> *Fair fa' your honest, sonsie face,*
> *Great Chieftain o' the Puddin-race!*
> *Aboon them a' ye tak your place,*
> *Painch, tripe, or thairm:*
> *Weel are ye wordy of a grace*
> *As lang's my arm.*

> *The groaning trencher there ye fill,*
> *Your hurdies like a distant hill,*
> *Your pin wad help to mend a mill*
> *In time o' need,*
> *While thro' your pores the dews distil*
> *Like amber bead.*

His knife see rustic Labour dight,
An' cut ye up wi' ready slight,
Trenching your gushing entrails bright,
Like onie ditch;
And then, O what a glorious sight,
Warm-reekin, rich!

Then, horn for horn, they stretch an' strive:
Deil tak the hindmost, on they drive,
Till a' their weel-swall'd kytes belyve
Are bent like drums;
Then auld Guidman, maist like to rive,
Bethankit hums.

Is there that owre his French ragout,
Or olio that was staw a sow,
Or fricassee wad mak her spew
Wi' perfect sconner,
Looks down wi' sneering, scornfu' view
On sic a dinner?

Poor devil! See him owre his trash,
As feckless as a wither'd rash,
His spindle shank a guid whip-lash;
His nieve a nit;
Thro' bluidy flood or field to dash,
O how unfit!

But mark the Rustic, haggis-fed,
The trembling earth resounds his tread.
Clap in his walie nieve a blade,
He'll mak it whissle;
An' legs an' arms, an' hands will sned,
Like taps o' thrissle.

Ye Pow'rs, wha mak mankind your care,
And dish them out their bill o' fare,
Auld Scotland wants nae skinking ware,
That jaups in luggies;
But, if ye wish her gratefu' prayer,
Gie her a haggis!

1786

'Cheers tae the Bard!'
TOASTS AND SPEECHES

Three principal toasts are offered at the traditional Burns Supper, though there's no reason why you shouldn't have more – as many as you or your guests might wish.

The Immortal Memory is indispensable, though: after all, it's what you're there to commemorate; there wouldn't have been any Burns suppers if it hadn't been for Burns. The speech doesn't have to be a work of scholarship, but it should at least give a nod to the significance of Burns' poetic works. Focus on what you think Burns and his poems mean to us today, his relevance to our society and time. It's worth at least taking a stab at some sort of analysis of a particular poem or a specific aspect of Burns' achievement: that way you can all get a fuller understanding of the poet and his work.

Once the Immortal Memory is complete, turn to face the great man's birthplace (with the help of the Burns Night app's handy compass, which always points to Alloway) as you make the toast: that will lend an authentic feel to the occasion.

LASSIES AND LADS

The Toast to the Lassies has had a chequered history, to say the least – but then Burns himself did in his dealings with the fair sex. The name of the speech itself implies a more complimentary toast than has sometimes been assumed. Too often it's been an excuse for self-satisfied bores to unburden themselves of their more misogynistic jokes and stories; but it really doesn't have to be that way, especially nowadays. It's supposed to be witty and irreverent, of course: there can be (should be, even) a certain amount of amiable point-scoring, given that the women can certainly be relied on to give as good as they get.

Be sure to include a link between your speech and Burns' poetry, though, by adding in a few apposite quotes – you'll find that there's no shortage. Find inspiration, for example, from this unflattering description of Tam o' Shanter's wife: *'Whare sits our sulky, sullen dame, / Gathering her brows like gathering storm, / Nursing her wrath to keep it warm.'* Or perhaps from this rather kinder quote, from 'Green Grow the Rashes': *'The sweetest hours that e'er I spend, / Are spent amang the lasses, O.'*

Any sister, wife, mother, daughter, girlfriend or granny can be appointed to give the Reply to the Toast to the Lassies. She gets the chance to turn the tables on the women's behalf. When preparing your Reply, consider Burns' own (comparatively enlightened) stance on women's rights and status and his views on their intellectual equality with men. Of particular interest may be Rabbie's 1792 poem, 'The Rights of Woman', a tongue-in-cheek squib that nevertheless concludes by proclaiming the 'Majesty of Woman!'

BETTER BLETHER

Giving toasts and speeches to a (possibly merry) room can be a daunting task: the key to success is knowing your audience, and remembering that you're trying to entertain them – not to air your own knowledge or critical expertise. It's not supposed to be a seminar. Short and sweet works well, since it keeps your audience interested; the more crisp and clear the points you make, the better – but if you do have colourful anecdotes, by all means use them.

Try to be engaging and to entertain. Not everyone was born with the gift of the gab, maybe, but with a bit of thought and planning – and a certain amount of judicious raiding of Burns' works (or the dictionary of quotations!) – you'll find it easier than you think to put together something interesting and entertaining. As with any speech, always remember to smile and make eye contact with those around you: they'll forgive you any small stumbles if they feel you're on their side. Above all, have fun: so long as you enjoy it, you'll find the audience will enjoy it, too. (And if you're really not confident you're the lad or lassie for the job, delegate to a guest instead.)

'Bawdy and Bonnie Burns'
THE INSULT AND COMPLIMENT FINDER

Do you, as toast-maker, feel bawdy enough to utter a scathing insult? Or does your speech-making style incline you more to bestowing a bonnie compliment? Either way, you can find inspiration in our 'Bawdy and Bonnie Burns Insult and Compliment Finder'. You'll find a randomised version on the app, if you're willing to risk improvising with it!

Mix and match the adjectives and nouns to create your own insult or compliment; you can even try to tailor it to the recipient, or else assign pairs of words to your guests and crowdsource the speech-making. Whether your opponent is a 'sulky mangled hav'rel', a 'big-belly'd ramgunshoch blockhead', or even a 'bonnie supple maid', this supply of ready-made, guaranteed-Burnsian insults and compliments will ensure that the evening's speeches aren't short of a witty remark or two. Some of the more obscure insults are missing from our glossary; it would be a shame to cramp your style.

INSULTS		COMPLIMENTS	
ADJECTIVES	NOUNS	ADJECTIVES	NOUNS
Auld	Blellum	*Beauteous*	Angel
Base	Blockhead	*Blissful*	Belle
Big-belly'd	Cadie	*Bonnie*	Bonnet
Blethering	Carlin	*Charming*	Burdie
Capricious	Caitiff	*Divine*	Dame
Chuffie	Coof	*Dove-like*	Dearie
Dim	Hav'rel	*Fairest*	Flower
Drunken	Hizzie	*Gentle*	Goddess
Hairum-scarium	Horse-leech	*Glimmering*	Jad
		Heavenly	Lass
Ill-tongu'd	Hurdie	*Pretty*	Maid
Mangled	Jads	*Supple*	Queen o' womankind
Pawkie	Skellum		
Ramgunshoch	Spunkie	*Sweet*	Rosebud
Rigwoodie	Sycophant		
Runkl'd	Thief		
Sleest	Tinkler		
Sulky	Trashtrie		
Tittlan	Warlock		
Ungentle	Witch		
Wither'd	Wretch		

'Ah, Tam! Ah, Tam! Thou'll Get thy Fairin'
TAM'S TALE

Written in the summer of 1790, for inclusion in the second volume of Francis Grose's *Antiquities of Scotland* the following year, 'Tam o' Shanter' turned out to be a poem for all time.

The story is straightforward enough: Tam, in Ayr for market day, stays too long in the pub as evening falls; he and his grey mare, Meg, then face a long and spooky ride home. Happening upon a dancing Sabbath of witches and warlocks, Tam stops and watches raptly until – stirred by the sight of one particularly appealing young witch in her 'cutty sark' (short shirt) – he cries out aloud, betraying his presence to this diabolical company. Fleeing suddenly for his life, he has a nightmarish ride, Meg at a headlong gallop, the evil crew in hot pursuit, until finally horse and rider escape over a bridge (evil spirits can't cross running water). Tam escapes unscathed; sadly, the same cannot be said for Meg, who loses her tail when it's grabbed by a witch as she hurtles frantically across the bridge.

THE INCOMPARABLE 'TAM'

'Tam o' Shanter' is unique in the British literary canon in its combination of rumbustious energy and stylistic poise; of gothic grotesqueness and good humour; of tavern jokes and sophisticated wit. The tone is real and fresh, and the verses career along with the rhythm of Tam's madcap ride. The poem is very much a product of the oral storytelling tradition, particularly in relation to the witches and warlocks, and the magical implications of Tam's drunken ride home. It is also one of the undoubted glories of Scots and (why stop there?) world literature.

The epic poem is reproduced here. Try reciting it yourself or split the recital amongst your guests (and for inspiration, listen to the performance by actor and musician Alasdair Macrae on the Burns Night app, which also has an autocue.)

Whichever way you hear 'Tam o' Shanter', it always adds another dimension to your Burns Night, driving home the dazzling scope of the Scottish Bard's poetic brilliance.

TAM O' SHANTER: A TALE

When chapman billies leave the street,
And drouthy neebors, neebors meet,
As market-days are wearing late,
An' folk begin to tak the gate;
While we sit bousing at the nappy,
And getting fou and unco happy,
We think na on the lang Scots miles,
The mosses, waters, slaps, and styles,
That lie between us and our hame,
Whare sits our sulky, sullen dame,
Gathering her brows like gathering storm,
Nursing her wrath to keep it warm.

This truth fand honest Tam o' Shanter,
As he frae Ayr ae night did canter,
(Auld Ayr, wham ne'er a town surpasses
For honest men and bonnie lasses.)

O Tam! had'st thou but been sae wise,
As ta'en thy ain wife Kate's advice!
She tauld thee weel thou was a skellum,
A blethering, blustering, drunken blellum;
That frae November till October,
Ae market-day thou was nae sober;
That ilka melder, wi' the miller,
Thou sat as lang as thou had siller;
That ev'ry naig was ca'd a shoe on,
The smith and thee gat roaring fou on;
That at the Lord's house, even on Sunday,
Thou drank wi' Kirkton Jean till Monday.
She prophesied that late or soon,
Thou would be found deep drown'd in Doon;
Or catch'd wi' warlocks in the mirk,
By Alloway's auld haunted kirk.

Ah, gentle dames! it gars me greet,
To think how mony counsels sweet,

How mony lengthen'd, sage advices,
The husband frae the wife despises!

But to our tale: Ae market-night,
Tam had got planted unco right;
Fast by an ingle, bleezing finely,
Wi' reaming swats, that drank divinely
And at his elbow, Souter Johnny,
His ancient, trusty, drouthy crony;
Tam lo'ed him like a very brither;
They had been fou for weeks thegither!
The night drave on wi' sangs and clatter
And ay the ale was growing better:
The landlady and Tam grew gracious,
Wi' favours secret, sweet and precious:
The Souter tauld his queerest stories;
The landlord's laugh was ready chorus:
The storm without might rair and rustle,
Tam did na mind the storm a whistle.

Care, mad to see a man sae happy,
E'en drown'd himsel' amang the nappy:
As bees flee hame wi' lades o' treasure,
The minutes wing'd their way wi' pleasure:

Kings may be blest, but Tam was glorious,
O'er a' the ills o' life victorious!

But pleasures are like poppies spread,
You seise the flower, its bloom is shed;
Or like the snow falls in the river,
A moment white – then melts for ever;
Or like the borealis race,
That flit ere you can point their place;
Or like the rainbow's lovely form
Evanishing amid the storm. –
Nae man can tether time or tide;
The hour approaches Tam maun ride;
That hour, o' night's black arch the key-stane,
That dreary hour he mounts his beast in;
And sic a night he taks the road in
As ne'er poor sinner was abroad in.

The wind blew as 'twad blawn its last;
The rattling showers rose on the blast;
The speedy gleams the darkness swallow'd
Loud, deep, and lang, the thunder bellow'd:
That night, a child might understand,
The Deil had business on his hand.

Weel mounted on his gray mare, Meg,
A better never lifted leg,
Tam skelpit on thro' dub and mire;
Despising wind, and rain, and fire.
Whyles holding fast his gude blue bonnet;
Whyles crooning o'er some auld Scots sonnet;
Whyles glow'ring round wi' prudent cares,
Lest bogles catch him unawares:
Kirk-Alloway was drawing nigh,
Whare ghaists and houlets nightly cry.

By this time he was cross the ford,
Whare, in the snaw, the chapman smoor'd;
And past the birks and meikle stane,
Whare drunken Charlie brak's neck-bane;
And thro' the whins, and by the cairn,
Whare hunters fand the murder'd bairn;
And near the thorn, aboon the well,
Whare Mungo's mither hang'd hersel'.
Before him Doon pours all his floods;
The doubling storm roars thro' the woods;
The lightnings flash from pole to pole;
Near and more near the thunders roll:
When, glimmering thro' the groaning trees,

Kirk-Alloway seem'd in a bleeze;
Thro' ilka bore the beams were glancing;
And loud resounded mirth and dancing.

Inspiring bold John Barleycorn!
What dangers thou canst make us scorn!
Wi' tippeny, we fear nae evil;
Wi' usquabae, we'll face the Devil!
The swats sae ream'd in Tammie's noddle,
Fair play, he car'd na deils a boddle.
But Maggie stood, right sair astonish'd,
Till, by the heel and hand admonish'd,
She ventured forward on the light;
And, vow! Tam saw an unco sight

Warlocks and witches in a dance;
Nae cotillion brent new frae France,
But hornpipes, jigs strathspeys, and reels,
Put life and mettle in their heels.
A winnock-bunker in the east,
There sat auld Nick, in shape o' beast;
A tousie tyke, black, grim, and large,
To gie them music was his charge:
He screw'd the pipes and gart them skirl,

Till roof and rafters a' did dirl. –
Coffins stood round, like open presses,
That shaw'd the dead in their last dresses;
And by some devilish cantraip sleight,
Each in its cauld hand held a light.
By which heroic Tam was able
To note upon the haly table,
A murderer's banes in gibbet-airns;
Twa span-lang, wee, unchristen'd bairns;
A thief new-cutted frae a rape,
Wi' his last gasp his gab did gape;
Five tomahawks, wi blude red-rusted;
Five scymitars, wi' murder crusted;
A garter, which a babe had strangled;
A knife, a father's throat had mangled,
Whom his ain son o' life bereft,
The grey-hairs yet stack to the heft;
[Three Lawyers' tongues, turned inside out,
Wi' lies seamed like a beggar's clout;
Three Priests' hearts, rotten black as muck,
Lay stinking, vile, in every neuk].

As Tammie glowr'd, amaz'd, and curious,
The mirth and fun grew fast and furious;

56

The piper loud and louder blew;
The dancers quick and quicker flew;
They reel'd, they set, they cross'd, they cleekit,
Till ilka carlin swat and reekit,
And coost her duddies to the wark,
And linket at it in her sark!

Now Tam, O Tam! had thae been queans,
A' plump and strapping in their teens,
Their sarks, instead o' creeshie flannen,
Been snaw-white seventeen hunder linnen!
Thir breeks o' mine, my only pair,
That ance were plush, o' guid blue hair,
I wad hae gi'en them off my hurdies,
For ae blink o' the bonie burdies!

But wither'd beldams, auld and droll,
Rigwoodie hags wad spean a foal,
Louping and flinging on a crummock,
I wonder did na turn thy stomach!
But Tam kend what was what fu' brawlie:
There was ae winsome wench and wawlie,
That night enlisted in the core,
(Lang after kend on Carrick shore;

For mony a beast to dead she shot,
An' perish'd mony a bonie boat,
And shook baith meikle corn and bear,
And kept the country-side in fear.)
Her cutty-sark, o' Paisley harn
That while a lassie she had worn,
In longitude tho' sorely scanty,
It was her best, and she was vauntie, –
Ah! little kend thy reverend grannie,
That sark she coft for her wee Nannie,
Wi' twa pund Scots, ('twas a' her riches),
Wad ever grac'd a dance of witches!

But here my Muse her wing maun cour;
Sic flights are far beyond her pow'r;
To sing how Nannie lap and flang,
(A souple jade she was, and strang),
And how Tam stood, like ane bewitch'd,
And thought his very een enrich'd;
Even Satan glowr'd, and fidg'd fu' fain,
And hotch'd and blew wi' might and main;
Till first ae caper, syne anither,
Tam tint his reason a' thegither,
And roars out, 'Weel done, Cutty-sark!'

And in an instant all was dark:
And scarcely had he Maggie rallied,
When out the hellish legion sallied.

As bees bizz out wi' angry fyke,
When plundering herds assail their byke;
As open pussie's mortal foes,
When, pop! she starts before their nose;
As eager runs the market-crowd,
When 'Catch the thief!' resounds aloud;
So Maggie runs, the witches follow,
Wi' mony an eldritch skriech and hollow.

Ah, Tam! ah, Tam! thou'll get thy fairin'!
In hell they'll roast thee like a herrin'!
In vain thy Kate awaits thy comin'!
Kate soon will be a woefu' woman!
Now, do thy speedy utmost, Meg,
And win the key-stane o' the brig;
There at them thou thy tail may toss,
A running stream they dare na cross.
But ere the key-stane she could make,
The fient a tail she had to shake!
For Nannie, far before the rest,
Hard upon noble Maggie prest,

And flew at Tam wi' furious ettle;
But little wist she Maggie's mettle –
Ae spring brought off her master hale,
But left behind her ain grey tail;
The carlin claught her by the rump,
And left poor Maggie scarce a stump.

No, wha this tale o' truth shall read,
Ilk man and mother's son take heed;
Whene'er to drink you are inclin'd,
Or cutty-sarks run in your mind,
Think! ye may buy joys o'er dear –
Remember Tam o' Shanter's mare.

1791

'Loud Resounded Mirth and Dancing'
MUSIC AND DANCE

It's fitting that Tam o' Shanter should have lost his head (and very nearly his life) at the sight of a ceilidh. Burns himself was a sucker for a session of music, song and dance. Between the bagpipes and the ceilidh, with its jigs, hornpipes, strathspeys, reels and all the rest of it, music still looms large in the Scottish identity. Burns Night isn't really Burns Night without these sounds.

You may have piped in your guests and the haggis with bagpipe music, and there will no doubt be some after-dinner medley fun, with the ceilidh band bringing your evening to a climactic close. In between, though, there's the opportunity to change the mood; to downshift a gear or enliven the proceedings with a sprinkling of Robert Burns' most famous songs. Some of these are Burns Supper staples: *Ae Fond Kiss* and *A Man's a Man for A' That* are popular choices (and ending the evening with *Auld Lang Syne* is just about obligatory, but we'll come to that). These works can be found in the next pages, along with several other popular songs and poems that can be incorporated into the evening.

But there are many more, just waiting to be discovered, if you're interested in exploring Burns' lyrical legacy – and hundreds, if not thousands, of different versions; many by great composers. Again, live voices add a special excitement, but there are endless recordings available as well. Of course, if neither you nor your friends feel up to solo performances, there's nothing to stop you all singing together, just so long as one of you is prepared to take a lead. A piano, with a halfway competent player, is great to have, of course – but it's by no means essential when you can all sing along with a recording, karaoke-style.

POETIC PRATFALLS

It's fun to have recitations (or readings), too: it makes sense to have these interspersed through the evening's proceedings, but a midway point is obviously an ideal time – perhaps to have a few. The more the merrier – and, conversely, it's a general rule with Burns Night that the less bashful you and your guests can be the better: it's worth doing everything you can to get people up on their feet performing poems. If they can do it well, that's great of course, but if they falter or stumble over the Scots, that's no problem by this time in the evening when everyone's – to put it tactfully – relaxed.

If you have young children amongst your guests, you may find they're more willing than their elders to lead the way. Many of Burns' lyrics (most obviously 'My Luve Is Like a Red, Red Rose') are short and simply expressed, easy to learn by heart – and even easier to read aloud; many were deliberately written in English, rather than in Scots. These include some of his most famous works: 'My Heart's in the Highlands', 'Flow Gently Sweet Afton' and many more.

In any case, you don't have to stick with Burns: other Scots like Robert Louis Stevenson wrote great verse with kids specifically in mind, as have more modern writers like Liz Lochhead, Carol Ann Duffy, Kathleen Jamie and Jackie Kay.

'THEY REEL'D, THEY SET, THEY CROSS'D, THEY CLEEKIT...'

Everyone loves a ceilidh: even people who don't think that they like dancing have often found themselves giddy and breathless – but completely converted – by the evening's end. So if you're in anything bigger than a bedsit room, push back the chairs and tables and clear the decks for dancing. Live music creates the most exciting and authentic atmosphere. The traditional ceilidh band boasts some or all of the following: fiddler, accordionist, keyboard player and percussionist. At a big event, there might be more than one of each – not to mention musicians with other instruments as well. For an added Scottish touch, why not get the bagpiper involved?

Whether or not a ceilidh is your usual choice for a night out, Burns Night is the time to let rip and enjoy the dances. There is nothing like *The Dashing White Sergeant*, *The Gay Gordons* and *Strip the Willow* for getting the blood pumping and the adrenalin going. A band member calls the steps, so everyone can be involved and, in many of the dances, partners are exchanged with every verse.

As with the bagpipes, it's not always going to be realistic to hire a ceilidh band. Again, though, there are countless CDs available. Many of these take you through the dances move by move, followed by a few full plays of the tune for you to have a go to – the next best thing to having your own band, complete with caller. The atmosphere won't be quite as buoyant as with a real live band, perhaps, but it'll still be a wonderful addition to the evening. As with all these things, a great deal depends on the attitudes of those taking part: the harder you all pitch in, the more fun you'll end up having.

'Thou Best and Dearest'
MOST POPULAR VERSES

These are some perennial favourites. What's yours?

AE FOND KISS

Ae fond kiss, and then we sever;
Ae fareweel, and then forever!
Deep in heart-wrung tears I'll pledge thee,
Warring sighs and groans I'll wage thee.

Who shall say that Fortune grieves him,
While the star of hope she leaves him?
Me, nae cheerfu' twinkle lights me;
Dark despair around benights me.

I'll ne'er blame my partial fancy:
Naething could resist my Nancy:
But to see her, was to love her;
Love but her, and love for ever.
Had we never lov'd sae kindly,
Had we never lov'd sae blindly!
Never met – or never parted,
We had ne'er been broken-hearted.
Fare-thee-weel, thou first and fairest!

Fare-thee-weel, thou best and dearest!
Thine be ilka joy and treasure,
Peace, Enjoyment, Love and Pleasure!

Ae fond kiss, and then we sever!
Ae fareweel, Alas, for ever!
Deep in heart-wrung tears I'll pledge thee,
Warring sighs and groans I'll wage thee.

1791

A MAN'S A MAN FOR A' THAT

Is there, for honest Poverty
That hings his head, an' a' that;
The coward-slave – we pass him by,
We dare be poor for a' that!
For a' that, an' a' that,
Our toils obscure, an' a' that,
The rank is but the guinea's stamp,
The Man's the gowd for a' that.

What though on hamely fare we dine,
Wear hoddin grey, an' a' that?
Gie fools their silks, and knaves their wine;
A Man's a Man' for a' that.
For a' that, and a' that,
Their tinsel show, an' a' that;
The honest man, tho' e'er sae poor,
Is king o' men for a' that.

Ye see yon birkie ca'd a lord,
Wha struts, an' stares, an' a' that;
Tho' hundreds worship at his word,
He's but a coof for a' that.
For a' that, an' a' that,

His ribband, star, an' a' that:
The man o' independent mind
He looks an' laughs at a' that.

A Prince can mak a belted knight,
A marquis, duke, an' a' that!
But an honest man's aboon his might,
Guid faith, he mauna fa' that!
For a' that, an' a' that,
Their dignities, an' a' that;
The pith o' Sense, an' pride o' Worth
Are higher rank than a' that.

Then let us pray that come it may,
As come it will for a' that,
That Sense and Worth o'er a' the earth
Shall bear the gree, an' a' that.
For a' that, an' a' that,
It's comin yet for a' that,
That Man to Man, the warld o'er
Shall brithers be for a' that.

1795

MY LUVE IS LIKE A RED, RED ROSE

O my Luve's like a red, red rose,
That's newly sprung in June;
O my Luve's like the melodie
That's sweetly play'd in tune.

As fair art thou, my bonnie lass,
So deep in luve am I;
And I will luve thee still, my Dear,
Till a' the seas gang dry.

Till a' the seas gang dry, my Dear,
And the rocks melt wi' the sun:
I will luve thee still, my dear,
While the sands o' life shall run.

And fare thee weel, my only Luve!
And fare thee weel, a while!
And I will come again, my Luve,
Tho' it were ten thousand mile!

1794

TO A LOUSE, ON SEEING ONE ON A LADY'S BONNET AT CHURCH

Ha! whare ye gaun, ye crowlan ferlie!
Your impudence protects you sairly:
I canna say but ye strunt rarely
Owre gauze and lace,
Tho' faith, I fear ye dine but sparely
On sic a place.

Ye ugly, creepan, blastet wonner,
Detested, shunn'd by saunt an' sinner,
How daur ye set your fit upon her –
Sae fine a lady!
Gae somewhere else and seek your dinner
On some poor body.

Swith! in some beggar's haffet squattle:
There ye may creep, and sprawl, and sprattle,
Wi' ither kindred, jumping cattle,

In shoals and nations;
Whare horn nor bane ne'er daur unsettle
Your thick plantations.

Now haud you there, ye're out o' sight,
Below the fatt'rels, snug an' tight,
Na, faith ye yet! ye'll no be right,
Till ye've got on it –
The vera tapmost, tow'ring height
O' Miss's bonnet.

My sooth! right bauld ye set your nose out,
As plump an' grey as onie grozet:
O for some rank, mercurial rozet,
Or fell, red smeddum,
I'd gie you sic a hearty dose o't,
Wad dress your droddum!

I wad na been surpris'd to spy
You on an auld wife's flainen toy;
Or aiblins some bit dubbie boy,
On 's wylecoat;
But Miss's fine Lunardi, fye!
How daur ye do't?

O Jenny, dinna toss your head,
An' set your beauties a' abroad!
Ye little ken what cursed speed
The blastie's makin:
Thae winks an' finger-ends, I dread,
Are notice takin!

O wad some Pow'r the giftie gie us
To see oursels as ithers see us!
It wad frae monie a blunder free us,
An' foolish notion:
What airs in dress an' gait wad lea'e us,
An ev'n Devotion!

1786

TO A MOUSE, ON TURNING HER UP IN
HER NEST WITH THE PLOUGH

Wee, sleekit, cowrin, tim'rous beastie,
O, what a panic's in thy breastie!
Thou need na start awa saw hasty
Wi' bickering brattle!
I wad be laith to rin an' chase thee,
Wi' murdering pattle!

I'm truly sorry Man's dominion
Has broken Nature's social union,
An' justifies that ill opinion
Which makes thee startle
At me, thy poor, earth-born companion
An' fellow mortal!

I doubt na, whyles, but thou may thieve;
What then? poor beastie, thou maun live!
A daimen icker in a thrave
'S a sma' request;
I'll get a blessin wi' the lave,
An' never miss't!

Thy wee-bit housie, too, in ruin!
Its silly wa's the win's are strewin!
An' naething, now, to big a new ane,
O' foggage green!
An' bleak December's win's ensuing,
Baith snell an' keen!

Thou saw the fields laid bare an' waste,
An' weary Winter comin fast,
An' cozie here, beneath the blast,
Thou thought to dwell,

Till crash! the cruel coulter past
Out thro' thy cell.

That wee bit heap o' leaves an' stibble,
Has cost thee monie a weary nibble!
Now thou's turned out, for a' thy trouble,
But house or hald,
To thole the Winter's sleety dribble,
An' cranreuch cauld!

But Mousie, thou art no thy lane,
In proving foresight may be vain:
The best-laid schemes o' Mice an' Men
Gang aft agley,
An' lea'e us nought but grief an' pain,
For promis'd joy!

Still thou art blest, compared wi' me!
The present only toucheth thee:
But Och! I backward cast my e'e,
On prospects drear!
An' forward, tho' I canna see,
I guess an' fear!

1785

'A Cup o' Kindness'
AULD LANG SYNE

No New Year's party is quite complete without a rousing chorus of *Auld Lang Syne*. This holds true far beyond the English- (or Scots-) speaking world. Most nations have their own translations for what is believed to be – after *Happy Birthday* – the world's most famous song.

It's certainly by some distance the best-known work of Robert Burns, so it naturally has its own special place at the Burns Night supper. Not just on account of its popularity, though: it's fitting because Burns Night is a time not only for celebrating the great man's 'Immortal Memory' but for remembering past gatherings and absent or departed friends. Guests traditionally sing *Auld Lang Syne* to mark these special bonds, standing in a circle, holding hands, crossing them over at the line 'There's a hand, my trusty fiere!'

'I DOUBT NA WHYLES, BUT THOU MAY THIEVE'

It's a great song, there's no doubt about it. Burns obviously thought so when he first heard it, for – whisper it – the claim that *Auld Lang Syne* was 'his' requires qualification. It's at very least arguable that he should be seen more as the song's editor than its author. As with several other of his works, it appears that he patched together phrases from the folk tradition and the popular Scots verse of previous generations.

It should be said that, in this, he wasn't doing anything new or unusual; neither was he the least bit furtive or underhand about it. People then took a much more free and easy attitude to issues of authorship, 'intellectual property' – and even that of 'originality'. The whole idea of copyright for published works was relatively new – and no one thought of its extending into what we now call the 'oral tradition'. If you heard a nice phrase in a ballad, folk song or children's rhyme and thought you could use it to make something better, you'd do so without any compunction or embarrassment – why wouldn't you?

And no one would dispute that Burns improved on what had come down to him through the folk tradition, or that he's responsible for the seamless whole we know and recite today. *Auld Lang Syne* stands as a towering testament to Burns' imagination and poetic skill, in bringing old and new together to produce a work that seems sure to go on speaking to all nations for all time.

AULD LANG SYNE

Should auld acquaintance be forgot
And never brought to mind?
Should auld acquaintance be forgot,
And auld lang syne!

For auld lang syne, my jo,
For auld lang syne,
We'll tak a cup o' kindness yet,
For auld lang syne.

And surely ye'll be your pint stowp!
And surely I'll be mine!
And we'll tak a cup o' kindness yet,
For auld lang syne.

For auld lang syne, my jo,
For auld lang syne,
We'll tak a cup o' kindness yet,
For auld lang syne.
We twa hae run about the braes,
And pou'd the gowans fine;
But we've wander'd mony a weary fitt,
Sin' auld lang syne.

For auld lang syne, etc.

We twa hae paidl'd in the burn,
Frae morning sun till dine;
But seas between us braid hae roar'd,
Sin' auld lang syne.

For auld lang syne, etc.

And there's a hand, my trusty fiere!
And gie's a hand o' thine!
And we'll tak a right gude-willie-waught,
For auld lang syne!

For auld lang syne, etc.

1796

Burns In Bits

PARTY GAMES AND MORE

Once the traditional elements of the evening are done, all there is left to do is enjoy the rest of the night. You can wow your fellow partygoers with your incredible knowledge of Burns' life and his role as a cultural inspirer.

For instance, did they know that Robert Burns' poem 'Comin' thro' the Rye' inspired the title of JD Salinger's *Catcher in the Rye*? Perhaps they did; but then you can impress them with your further knowledge of Burns, with some of the following little-known factoids.

INSPIRED BY BURNS

* Asked by an interviewer in 2008 to name the lyric that had inspired him most, Bob Dylan chose Burns' 'My Luve is Like a Red, Red Rose'.

* John Steinbeck's *Of Mice and Men* took its title from Burns' 'To a Mouse' ('The best-laid schemes o' mice and men / Gang aft agley'); Robbie Williams paraphrased the line in the lyrics of *Summertime*.

* Michael Jackson (and David Gest) recorded an album's worth of Robert Burns' works with a contemporary musical setting. It was never released, but Gest donated the recordings to the Robert Burns Birthplace Museum in Alloway.

* Among the many musicians who composed versions of Burns' songs in the early nineteenth century were such masters as Josef Haydn and Ludwig van Beethoven.

* 'A Man's A Man for A' That' was chosen as the poem to open the Scottish Parliament in 1999.

* Burns had the Soviet Union's full stamp of approval. Rabbie was heralded as the 'people's poet' by the Soviet authorities, and his poems were taught in Russian schools. While the Royal Mail has issued three sets of stamps honouring the wordsmith, it was the Soviet Union that got there first – issuing the first commemorative Burns stamp to mark the 160th anniversary of his death in 1956.

BURNS TRIVIA

* For all Burns' secular prose, there is never a word spoken against religion in any of his work.

* Whilst he railed against the hypocrisy of certain individuals, he was an ardent attendant of the Church to the last.

* Burns' sexual adventures were covered up in the century or so after his death. *It wisnae whit ye're thinkin'!*

* When, in 1930, Catherine Carswell published the first full and frank biography of his life, she received a bullet through the post.

* Shoe size isn't linked to other important male dimensions, medical research suggests – despite the myths. Burns would have taken a UK size 8.

* The tune we all know for *Auld Lang Syne* is not in fact the one Burns originally envisaged. You can hear that one sung beautifully by Kirsty Grace on the Burns Night app – or else if you can brave the film version of *Sex and the City* (2008).

* The writer of 'My Luve is Like a Red, Red Rose' produced far raunchier verses, too. Much of this 'Blue Burns', collected in *Merry Muses of Caledonia*, remained banned in Britain until as late as 1965.

* In November 2009, Glasgow University students set what was believed to be a new world record: singing *Auld Lang Syne* simultaneously in forty-one different languages.

* Ayr United football club and its supporters call themselves the 'Honest Men' after a verse in 'Tam o' Shanter'. ('Auld Ayr, wham ne'er a toun surpasses / For honest men and bonnie lasses.')

* An average of four academic books on Burns have been published every single year since he died in 1796.

* There are at least sixty statues and monuments to Burns worldwide – more than there are for any other non-religious figures, apart from Queen Victoria and Christopher Columbus.

* Burns 'lost his head' in Timaru, New Zealand, in February 2012, when vandals decapitated his statue in the town's botanical gardens.

* Baby Burns very nearly didn't make it to manhood: the family cottage partially collapsed on him and mother Agnes just a few days after he was born in 1759.

* The Burns Federation, based in Kilmarnock,

recognises up to 400 affiliated clubs. Many thousands of more informal Burns Suppers are held around the world each year.

* Maxwell Burns, the poet's youngest son, was born on the very day of his father's funeral. Mother Jean Armour couldn't make it to the kirk.

* Burns first crossed the Final Frontier in 2010, when British-born US astronaut Nick Patrick took a collection of his poems into space. *Nae wonder there's a Klingon Auld Lang Syne!*

DO YOU 'GET' BURNS?... HANDY HINTS

Despite what any self-respecting Scot will tell the English, most people need a little help interpreting even the best-known poems.

TO A MOUSE

* *The best laid schemes o' Mice and Men / Gang aft agley*: 'The most carefully laid plans often go wrong'

TO A LOUSE

* *O wad some Pow'r the giftie gie us / To see oursels as ithers see us*: 'O, would some Power the small gift give us to see ourselves as others see us'

ADDRESS TO A HAGGIS

* *Fair fa' your honest, sonsie face, / Great Chieftain o' the Puddin-race!*: 'Fair and full is your honest, jolly face, great chieftain of the sausage race!'

* *Till a' their weel-swall'd kytes belyve / Are bent like drums; / Then auld Guidman, maist like to rive, / Bethankit hums"* 'Till all their well-swollen bellies by-and-by are bent like drums; then old head of the table, most like to burst, 'The grace!' hums'

* *Auld Scotland wants nae skinking ware, / That jaups in luggies; / But, if ye wish her gratefu' prayer, / Gie her a haggis!*: 'Old Scotland wants no watery stuff that splashes in small dishes; but, if you wish her grateful prayers, give her [Scotland] a haggis!'

A wee bit lost in translation?

AULD LANG SYNE

* *For auld lang syne, my jo...*: 'For old long ago, my sweetheart...'

* *We'll tak a right guid willie waught*: 'We'll take a good, deep draught of good cheer'.

TAM O 'SHANTER

* *When chapman billies leave the street / And drouthy neebors, neebors meet*: 'When market traders go

inside, and thirsty neighbours get together.'

* *Til ilka carlin swat and reekit, / And cast her duddies to the wark/and linket at it in her sark*: 'Till every witch sweated and steamed and threw her clothing to the floor and went to it in her slip.'

A MAN'S A MAN FOR A' THAT

* *Is there for honest poverty, / That hings his heid an' a' that:* 'Is there an honest man who'd hang his head in shame at being poor…?'

CA' THE YOWES TO THE KNOWES

* *Ca' the yowes to the knowes / Ca' them whare the heather grows / Ca' them whare the burnie rowes / My bonie Dearie:* 'Drive the ewes to the knolls, drive them where the heather grows, drive them where the stream runs, my lovely dear!' *Annie, Corrina and Karine sing this yin like angels on ma app*

THE KEEKIN' GLASS

* *How daur ye ca' me 'Howlet-face', / Ye blear-e'ed, wither'd spectre? / Ye only spied the keekin-glass, / An' there ye saw your picture.* 'How dare you call me 'Owl-face', you bleary-eyed, withered ghost? You only looked in the mirror – and saw your reflection.'

Dinnae Ken?
GLOSSARY

aboon	*above*	duddies	*old clothes*
aiblins	*perhaps*	eldritch	*supernatural*
bauld	*bold*	fient	*fiend, devil*
bickering	*hurrying*	fient a	*not a, none*
blellum	*babbler*	fou	*full, drunk*
boddle	*small coin*	gang	*to go*
bore	*a recess*	gowd	*gold*
brak's	*broke his*	haffet	*temple (forehead)*
breeks	*trousers*	haly	*holy*
brent	*straight/steep*	hoddin grey	*homespun cloth*
cabtraip	*magic*	hotch'd	*jerked*
claught	*seized*	hurdies	*buttocks*
coft	*bought*	ingle	*fire, hearth*
coost	*discarded*	kytes	*bellies*
cranreuch	*frost*	laith	*loath*
creeshie	*greasy*	lap	*leapt*
crowlin	*crawling*	lo'ed	*loved*
crummock	*stocky*	maist	*most, almost*
cutty sark	*short shirt*	mark	*a coin*
daimen icker	*odd ear of corn*	maunna	*mustn't*
dub	*puddle, slush*	meikle	*much, great*

melder	*a grinding corn*	squattle	*settle*
mettle	*spirited, lively*	startle	*to course*
mind	*remember*	staw	*to sicken*
naig	*a nag*	strunt	*swagger*
nappy	*ale*	swats	*ale*
neuk	*corner*	tak	*take*
nieve	*fist*	tauld	*told*
owre	*over*	thairm	*small guts*
rair	*roar*	thole	*to suffer*
rair	*severe(ly)*	thrave	*24 sheaves (grain)*
rigwoodie	*lean*	tint	*lost*
sark	*undershirt*	twa	*two*
saunt	*saint*	unco	*remarkable*
skinking	*watery*	walie	*large*
smoor'd	*smothered*	ware	*spend, bestow*
snaw	*snow*	waught	*large draught*
snell	*bitter*	waulie	*jolly*
sonsie	*pleasant*	weel	*well*
souple	*supple*	wham	*whom*
souter	*cobbler*	winnock-bunker	*window seat*
spean	*to wean*	wordy	*worthy*
spring	*tune, dance*	yon	*yonder*

Whaur tae Git Mair
FURTHER READING

* A comprehensive and witty guide to celebrating Burns Night: McGinn, Clark, *The Ultimate Burns Supper Book: A Practical (but Irreverent) Guide to Scotland's Greatest Celebration*. Edinburgh: Luath Press Ltd; illustrated edition (2007).

* A collection of stories about the history and development of Burns Suppers: Cairney, John, *Immortal Memories*. Edinburgh: Luath Press Ltd; new edition (2012).

* Scotland's favourite cartoon family provides a humorous but very useful step-by-step guide to planning and organising your own Burns Supper: *The Broons' Burns Night*. Glasgow: Waverley Books Ltd (2008).

* A comprehensive collection of Burns' poems and songs, with scholarly background information: Noble, Andrew and Patrick Scott Hogg: *The Canongate Burns*. Edinburgh: Canongate (reprint edition, 2011).

* A collection of some of Burns' best-known works, accompanied by annotations, explanations and glossary: Wilkie, George Scott & Robert Burns, *Selected Works of Robert Burns: Verse, Explanation and Glossary*. Glasgow: Neil Wilson Publishing (1999).

* The poems and songs of Robert Burns in a facsimile edition, with notes and glossary: Burns, Robert, *Complete Poems and Songs of Robert Burns*. Glasgow: Geddes & Grosset (2002).

* A selection of verse chosen personally and introduced by Ian Rankin: Burns, Robert, *Poems of Robert Burns Selected by Ian Rankin*. London: Penguin Classics (2008).

* A leading Scottish actor and Burns aficionado hand-picks and introduces sixty of his favourite poems: Cairney, John, *The Luath Burns Companion*. Edinburgh: Luath Press Ltd (2001).

Published by Saraband
Suite 202, 98 Woodlands Road
Glasgow, G3 6HB, Scotland
www.saraband.net

Copyright © Saraband 2013

All rights reserved. No part of this publication may be
reproduced, stored in a retrieval system, or transmitted,
in any form or by any means, electronic, mechanical,
photocopying, recording, or otherwise, without first
obtaining the written permission of the copyright
owner.

ISBN: 978-190864319-3

Printed in the EU on paper from sustainably
managed sources.

1 3 5 7 9 10 8 6 4 2

THANKS
Special thanks to contributors Michael Kerrigan and
Sophie Franklin, and for design and illustrations to
Chloe van Grieken. Cover design and image based on the
Burns Night app: Scott Smyth, www.ithinkitsnice.com
Thanks also to Craig Hillsley, Pete Murray, and every-
one who helped make the app, especially Kirsty, Graeme,
Sara, Alistair, Aly, Annie, Karine, Corrina, Stephanie,
Stephen and all at Toads Caravan and IDAC.

THE APP
http://saraband.net/history-culture/275-burns-night-app